Festivals *of the* World

CHINA

Gareth Stevens Publishing
MILWAUKEE

Written by
COLIN CHEONG

Edited by
ELIZABETH BERG

Designed by
LOO CHUAN MING

DF   JP EC

First published in North America in 1997 by
Gareth Stevens Publishing
1555 North RiverCenter Drive, Suite 201
Milwaukee, Wisconsin 53212 USA

For a free color catalog describing Gareth
Stevens' list of high-quality books and multimedia
programs, call
1-800-542-2595 (USA)
or 1-800-461-9120 (Canada).
Gareth Stevens Publishing's Fax: (414) 225-0377.
See our catalog, too, on the World Wide Web:
http://gsinc.com

© **TIMES EDITIONS PTE LTD 1997**
Originated and designed by
Times Books International
an imprint of Times Editions Pte Ltd
Times Centre, 1 New Industrial Road
Singapore 536196
Printed in Singapore

Library of Congress Cataloging-in-Publication Data:
Cheong, Colin.
China / by Colin Cheong.
p. cm. — (Festivals of the world)
Includes bibliographical references and index.
Summary: Describes how the culture of China is
reflected in its many festivals.
ISBN 0-8368-1681-1 (lib. binding)
1. Festivals—China—Juvenile literature. 2.
China—Social life and customs—Juvenile
literature. [1. Festivals—China. 2. China—Social
life and customs.] I. Title. II. Series.
GT4883.A2C484 1997
394.2'6951—dc20
96-32618

1 2 3 4 5 6 7 8 9 99 99 98 97

CONTENTS

It's Festival Time . . .

The word for "festival" in Chinese is 节日 [JYEH-reh]. (Didn't think you could read Chinese, did you?) The Chinese have been celebrating these festivals for thousands of years, and do they have lots of stories to tell about them! So come on and find out all about dragons, and the lady in the moon, and how to take care of ghosts. It's 节日 time in China . . .

WHERE'S CHINA?

China lies in the middle of Asia, between India in the west, and Korea and Japan in the east. There are rolling hills, wide plains, and high plateaus in China. The soil is rich in the eastern part, and farming is one of the most important activities there. That is where most of the people live. The southwest is covered with high mountains, and there are many deserts in the north. Few people live in these areas. There are many different climates in China. In the south, it is as warm as Hawaii, while in some northern regions, it is as cold as Alaska.

Who are the Chinese?

About one in every five people in the world lives in China. The earliest Chinese people lived around the Huanghe [hwang-HEH], or Yellow River, where the land is good for farming. For a long time, China was divided into warring states before being united under one emperor. There were also many times when China was conquered by foreigners.

A young boy from Shanghai, the second largest city in China (Beijing is the biggest). There are more people in China than in any other country in the world.

RUSSIAN FEDERATION

MONGOLIA

TAKLAMAKAN DESERT

Harbin

GOBI DESERT

GREAT WALL

BEIJING

SEA OF JAPAN

KOREA

TIBET

HIMALAYA MOUNTAINS

NEPAL

MOUNT EVEREST

Huanghe (Yellow River)

YELLOW SEA

JAPAN

BHUTAN

Chengdu

Shanghai

E A S T C H I N A S E A

INDIA   **BANGLADESH**

Yang Zi River

YUNNAN

•Guilin

FUJIAN

MYANMAR   **VIETNAM**   **LAOS**

HONG KONG

TAIWAN

CHINA   N

Most of the people in China are **Han Chinese**, but there are also 55 other groups. The Zhuang, Bai, Dai, Tibetans, and Mongolians are just a few. These people mostly live in the desert and mountain areas. Many Chinese have moved to other countries, such as Taiwan, Singapore, and the United States. They are called **Overseas Chinese**. Most Chinese follow a mixture of **Buddhism** and **Taoism**, but some of the smaller groups are **Muslim**.

The Great Wall of China was built many centuries ago to stop China's enemies from coming in. It runs for thousands of miles across northern China.

WHEN'S THE 节日?

That means "When's the Festival?" And it isn't an easy question to answer. China uses two types of calendars—the Gregorian calendar (the one we use) and a **lunar** calendar. The Gregorian calendar is used for things like work and school, while the lunar calendar is used for most festivals. Chinese festivals do not always fall on the same date or even the same month on the Gregorian calendar.

Meet you on the moon on page 22.

It's party time! Come to the Lantern Festival on page 12.

SPRING

- ✪ **CHINESE NEW YEAR** (1st day of 1st month)
- ✪ **DAI WATER SPLASHING FESTIVAL** (2nd day of 1st month)—Dai people splash water on each other to shower blessings and wish happiness. The more water, the more good wishes.
- ✪ **LANTERN FESTIVAL** (15th day of 1st month)
- ✪ **QING MING** (Pure Brightness Festival)
- ✪ **BIRTHDAY OF TIAN HOU, GODDESS OF THE SEA** (23rd day of 3rd month) Particularly popular among sailors, her festival is a big event in San Francisco, Hong Kong, and Taiwan. There are lion dancers, stiltwalkers, acrobats, and parades.

Come celebrate New Year's with us in Tibet on page 24.

SUMMER

⊛ **DRAGONBOAT FESTIVAL**
(5th day of 5th month)

AUTUMN

⊛ **THE COWHERD AND THE WEAVING MAID FESTIVAL**
(7th day of 7th month)—A women's festival, with sewing competitions to honor women's work.
⊛ **HUNGRY GHOSTS FESTIVAL** (15th day of 7th month)
⊛ **MID-AUTUMN FESTIVAL** (15th day of 8th month)
⊛ **DOUBLE-NINTH FESTIVAL** (9th day of 9th month)—A day to climb hills, have picnics, and drink chrysanthemum wine. Celebrates the coming of cold weather.
⊛ **NATIONAL DAY**—Huge parades and celebrations in Beijing to celebrate the birthday of the People's Republic of China.

WINTER

⊛ **WINTER SOLSTICE FESTIVAL**—The Thanksgiving Day of the Chinese calendar. Time to cook Tang Yuan (look at page 30).

Slither on over to page 14 for a dragon dance.

CHINESE NEW YEAR

Firecrackers, loud drumming, and clashing cymbals welcome the biggest festival on the Chinese calendar. This is the Spring Festival, or Chinese New Year, as it is traditionally known. For three days, the whole country shuts down. And then the celebration goes on for two weeks!

Cleaning and cooking

Before the New Year, you must give your house a good cleaning to get rid of all the bad luck collected in the past year. Then you can't sweep the house during the first days of the new year or you'll sweep all the new luck away! Also before the festival, you must prepare enough food to last at least three days because using a knife during the first days of the new year "cuts off" good luck. More importantly, you must pay off all your debts and settle all your quarrels with the neighbors so you can start fresh with the new year.

This girl is dressed up in her New Year's best. For the New Year, everyone dresses in bright colors, especially red because it is **auspicious**.

The Kitchen God is sent off

A week before the New Year, many people prepare a big feast for the Kitchen God. Who's the Kitchen God?

Once there was an evil man who left his wife for a younger woman. His new wife spent all his money and left him to beg for his food. When he was begging, he came to the house of a kind widow, who gave him food. When he saw that the widow was his first wife, he was so ashamed he jumped into the oven and burned. Because he saw his mistake, he was made the Kitchen God. (Or so the story goes. Some people say the Kitchen God is really an old woman.)

All year long, the Kitchen God watches over the fortunes of the family from his place in the kitchen. Then on the 23rd day of the last month of the year, he is given a feast and sent off to report on the family to the Jade Emperor, the highest god of Taoism. But before he goes, his mouth is smeared with honey so that he'll have only sweet things to say. (Or, some people say, so he won't be able to say anything at all.)

This wishes you prosperity in the coming year. Say, "Gong xi fa cai" [KONG tsee FAH chy].

For the New Year, older family members give children red envelopes with money inside, called **hongbao** [hong pow]. By the end of the holiday, you could get quite a bit of money from parents, grandparents, aunts, uncles, and others.

People put up lots of decorations for the New Year. The most popular are long strips of red paper with wishes of good luck written with a special brush. These are hung next to the doors.

Keeping monsters away

Everything is decorated in red for the New Year. There's a story behind that. A long time ago, there was a terrible monster called the *nian* that came at the end of every winter and ate everyone in sight in this one village. Then finally a wise man told the people that the monster was afraid of three things: noise, lights, and the color red. So they lit a bonfire, set off fireworks, and painted their doors red. From then on, the nian no longer bothered them. Now every New Year, people decorate their houses with red banners to protect against evil spirits. And setting off firecrackers is one of the favorite parts of the New Year celebration.

Children made up and ready to take part in a New Year parade. Many people go to see a fortuneteller on New Year's Day to find out what the year will bring. You could do your horoscope—find out how on page 26.

Rich foods and healthy words

Chinese New Year is a time when everyone is careful to say and do only nice things that will bring luck to the family in the next year. At the big meal on New Year's Eve, each dish has a name that brings to mind health or riches, like "Broth of Prosperity" or "Silvery Threads of Longevity." People like to eat candied **kumquats** because the first character in the Chinese name for kumquats means "gold." Another traditional food is meat dumplings. Some of the dumplings have copper coins cooked in them to bring luck. Everyone goes around wishing everyone else "Gong xi fa cai," which means "Wishing you prosperity." It is a time to be thoughtful and kind to everyone.

On New Year's Eve, the family gets together for a big dinner. That night the children stay up late. The longer they stay up, the longer their parents will live. For the next three days, people visit friends and relatives.

Think about this

Do you have any special beliefs about things to do on New Year's Day to bring luck in the next year? Many cultures have traditions of things that may bring good luck. For instance, many Americans believe they should eat black-eyed peas on New Year's Day.

THE LANTERN FESTIVAL

Fifteen days after the beginning of the Chinese New Year comes the first full moon of the year. Of course, it's time to celebrate! This is the Feast of the First Full Moon, also known as the Lantern Festival. The Lantern Festival began as a celebration of the light and warmth of the sun after winter. Now it is the last night of the New Year festival. People go out to look at the hundreds of lanterns hanging on the streets. The lanterns come in all sorts of shapes—boxes, globes, animals, and many others. Acrobats, jugglers, stiltwalkers, and other performers walk around the streets.

A girl gets her dad's advice on picking out a lantern. In Fujian Province, families used to light up as many lanterns as there were people in the family. If they wanted more children, they would light extra lanterns.

Remember to feed the lions

Lion dancers are a favorite all through the New Year and Lantern Festivals. Two young men from a **martial arts** school hide under the costume. They make the lion jump around, lie down, and roll over. To make it rear up on its hind legs, the front man jumps on the other's shoulders. Other people from the school beat on large drums and gongs, making a lot of noise. People invite lion dancers to come to their homes or shops to bring good luck in the next year. They put out some oranges and hongbao. The lion "eats" the oranges and hongbao and spits out the peel. The money from the hongbao will be used to support the school.

Acrobats and "dry boat" performers in Beijing. In dry boat plays, performers dress up in costumes that hide their legs and look like a boat. They pretend to be a boy and girl picking lotus flowers on a lake. This celebrates love and springtime.

Watch out for the lion!

13

Left: These masked figures are dressed up in their best clothes for the Lantern Festival. Look at that string of firecrackers! (It's not real, of course.)

Below: The Chinese dragon has the body of a snake, the head, mane, and tail of a horse, the paws of a dog, the horns of a deer, the scales and whiskers of fish, and the wings of a bird. Long ago, before China was one country, different tribes worshiped different animals. When the tribes were united, they joined parts of their animals into a single creature—the dragon.

Enter the dragon

The high point of the festivities is the dragon dance. The dragon is made out of paper or silk stretched over a bamboo frame. It is held up on poles by a dozen or more people who run together, making the dragon wind through the streets. One person holds a yellow globe for the dragon to chase. This is supposed to be the sun. If the dragon catches it, the sun will go out. But that has never happened. Instead, the dragon dance ends in a burst of fireworks. Long ago, people believed the dragon was in charge of clouds, rain, and rivers. The dragon dance celebrates the spring rain and the sun.

Bai girls perform a dance for the Lantern Festival in Yunnan Province. Many of the different peoples in China celebrate the same festivals as the Han Chinese.

Dragons abroad

In recent years, traditional festivals are celebrated quietly in China. People stay at home and have special meals with their family. This is because the government of China doesn't approve of these old customs. But the Overseas Chinese like to have big celebrations of their traditional festivals. The biggest dragon parade in the world is held in San Francisco every year.

Think about this

You can find dragons in almost every culture in the world. In Europe, Christian saints used to fight evil dragons. But in many other parts of the world, dragons are good creatures. In Africa and India, they sustain the world, and in Mexico the "plumed serpent," which looks a lot like a dragon, was an important god. Isn't it strange to find the same imaginary creature all over?

GHOST FESTIVALS

In Chinese culture, older relatives must be treated with respect and courtesy—even after they are dead. Many Chinese believe that after someone dies, their spirit lives on and knows what is happening in the world of the living. Spirits are powerful, so people try to make them happy by remembering them, offering them food, and burning incense. If an **ancestor**'s spirit is pleased, he or she might do you a favor. But spirits who are unhappy can make bad things happen.

Qing Ming

The Qing Ming [CHING ming] Festival is especially for remembering ancestors and making sure they are happy in their world. People offer food to the dead. They also burn paper money and other offerings. Burning something sends its spirit to the spirit world, where the dead can use it.

Leaving food for an ancestor. Qing Ming is one of the few holidays that is on the Gregorian calendar. It falls on April 4.

16

How did it get started?

Qing Ming means "Pure Brightness." The festival was originally a celebration of springtime. People celebrated by going out into the countryside to walk on the new grass. Then, because Qing Ming was a good time to go out into the countryside, people stopped to clean graves in the hills around the village.

A good time to fly a kite

Qing Ming is a time to rejoice in life. One activity is especially popular—kite flying. Kites have a special place in Chinese history. Long ago, according to legend, the states of Chu and Han were at war. Xin [tsin], the Han general, made a kite big enough for a warrior to ride in. The warrior used the kite to fly over the Chu camp singing Chu songs. Hearing songs from home made the Chu warriors so sad that they gave up and went home.

Bai people in Yunnan Province making offerings to their ancestors.

The dragon kite is a Chinese invention. It is difficult to fly, but quite spectacular to see.

When the hungry ghosts come to visit

Some Chinese believe that on the first day of the seventh lunar month the gates of hell are opened, and the spirits are allowed to wander in our world for a month. There are many spirits who have no one to offer them food and presents. These spirits may be angry and make trouble at this time of year, so people leave offerings for the stray ghosts. They leave food and incense by the roadside (it isn't wise to invite hungry spirits into your home). And they burn paper spirit money so the ghosts will have some spending money in the other world. This is called the Hungry Ghosts Festival.

Sticks of incense, called joss sticks, are burned to take prayers up to the spirit world. At funerals the Chinese often burn paper models of things the dead person might need, such as cars, houses, or money. Sometimes these are quite big and fancy.

Chinese opera is very popular, especially during Qing Ming. Sometimes performances are put on for the spirits. Chinese opera is quite different from Western opera. It includes songs, speaking, mime, dance, and acrobatics. Actors wear colorful costumes and masks.

Think about this

Halloween is quite a lot like the Hungry Ghosts Festival. Both are days when the dead are allowed to return to the world of the living. To keep them happy, you offer them a treat. Even if you don't believe in ghosts, you probably still give them something on Halloween.

DRAGONBOATS AND MOONCAKES

An old man stands in a boat floating on a deep river. Holding a heavy rock, he steps overboard, sinking quickly into the water. This is the story of Qu Yuan [chu you-EN], who killed himself because he couldn't stand to see his country ruined by poor leaders. The people of a nearby village went out in their boats to search for him, but they were too late. In great sorrow, they threw rice into the water to feed the man's hungry spirit. Then one day, his spirit returned and told them that the river dragon was eating all the food meant for him. He told the villagers to wrap the rice in leaves, shaping it like a small pyramid. Today people eat these rice dumplings at the Dragonboat Festival to remember Qu Yuan.

The leader of the winning boat raises his hands in the victory sign.

The Dragonboat Festival

The Dragonboat Festival takes place on the fifth day of the fifth lunar month, around midsummer. It probably started as a festival to celebrate the planting of the rice crop and to pray for a good rainfall. At that time, people believed that dragons controlled rivers and rain. They put offerings in the river so that the dragons would bring rain for their crops.

The highlight of the festival today is the dragonboat races. Dragonboats are long, narrow boats with a carved dragon's head at one end and a tail at the other. Up to 80 rowers paddle together. A leader shouts directions and sets the rhythm for the rowers using a large drum. The races are very noisy and exciting. Teams try to trick each other into a wrong move. Fights often break out between teams.

Dragonboat races are very competitive, and boats often turn over, much to the amusement of cheering spectators on the shore.

Long ago, people put offerings to the dragon gods in the rivers so that they would bring rain.

The Mid-Autumn Festival

The other festival that comes from the rice-growing cycle is the Mid-Autumn Festival. The Mid-Autumn Festival was once a day of thanksgiving for the rice harvest. It was an outdoor festival when people went out to the valleys and mountains to hike and picnic. Today the Mid-Autumn Festival is still spent outdoors, but now it is a celebration of the moon and the beauty of autumn.

According to the Chinese calendar, autumn falls on the seventh, eighth, and ninth months of the year. The Mid-Autumn Festival takes place on the 15th day of the eighth month, at the middle of autumn on the night of the full moon. On this night, the moon is at its roundest and brightest. It is a time to sit outside with friends and family, enjoy the moonlight, and eat mooncakes.

People harvesting rice in the beautiful Guilin region of China. The Mid-Autumn Festival takes place after the harvest, when farmers have free time to enjoy the cool autumn weather and the beauty of nature.

Have some mooncakes

Most mooncakes are brown, but some are white or even green. The most popular mooncakes have fillings made of egg yolk, lotus seed paste, or coconut.

The most common mooncakes are those with a brown skin and a sweet brown paste filling, but there are many different kinds—some sweet, some not. Mooncakes used to come in all sorts of shapes—**pagodas**, horses, fish, and other animals. Today they are usually round, with Chinese symbols in the middle.

Mooncakes save the day

Mooncakes are the heroes of a rebellion against the **Mongols** when China was under Mongol rule. The rebel army commander sent mooncakes to the people of one town a few days before the Mid-Autumn Festival. On the night of the festival, the people found notes in the mooncakes telling them to rise up and kill the Mongols at midnight. When the time came, the people attacked. The rebel army joined them, and the city was freed from Mongol rule.

Here's the lady in the moon holding a lantern.

The lady in the moon

There are many legends about the moon that people remember at the Mid-Autumn Festival. Here's the story of the lady in the moon. A long time ago, 10 suns suddenly appeared in the sky. The heat was terrible. The emperor ordered one of his best archers, Hou Yi, to shoot down the extra suns. Hou Yi shot down all but one. The queen of the immortals rewarded him with a pill that would let him live forever, but he had to wait for 12 months before he took the pill. One day while he was out, his wife, Chang Er, found the pill. She ate it and suddenly was able to fly. To escape her husband's anger, she flew to the moon, where she still lives today. Hou Yi flew to the sun. Since then, they see each other once a month when the moon is full.

TIBETAN NEW YEAR

The Tibetans have a very old culture that is quite different from Chinese culture. About 40 years ago, Tibet became part of China, but the Tibetans still keep a lot of their own traditions. One of these is Losar, the Tibetan New Year. In some ways, Losar is a little like Chinese New Year. Before the New Year, the house must be thoroughly cleaned and special meals prepared for the New Year's Day feast. Visiting friends is a big part of the celebration. But there are also traditions that are only followed in Tibet.

Let's dance

Tibetans follow their own type of Buddhism, called **Lamaism**. Their religion is very important to them. Most of their celebrations take place in the temple. For part of the New Year's celebrations, monks dress in masks and costumes. They put on dances at the temple to show the struggle between good and evil. It takes a lot of practice to do these dances. According to legend, one monk was able to make rocks explode and set robes on fire through his dancing.

Two monks perform a dance for the New Year celebrations.

Sweeping away the demons

Tibetans have a special practice to get rid of any demons that might have settled in their house over the year. On the last night of the year, the house is swept and the dirt left in a pile in the corner. On top they put little models of demons made out of dough. Then the women rebraid their hair and everyone gets dressed in their new clothes. They all sit down to eat a special soup.

After they have finished eating, everyone in the family helps to pick up the pile of dirt and the demons. They carry it all outside to a big fire. All the neighbors bring their piles of dirt, too. They throw it all on the fire, and everyone shouts and sets off fireworks to scare the demons back to their world.

Thangkas [THANG-kas] are paintings on fabric made in a special way. The hanging of the thangka before a festival is an important ceremony. Some are so big that it takes dozens of monks to carry them out of the room where they are kept.

The second day of the new year is full of religious ceremonies. Here a monk collects money for the temple.

THINGS FOR YOU TO DO

The Chinese believe that each year is ruled by one of 12 animals. People have the characteristics of the animal that ruled the year they were born. Find out what kind of animal you are by looking for the year you were born. Then read about what that sign is like. Does the description fit? (The little Chinese characters give the name of the animal in Chinese.)

RATS are bright, sociable, happy, and charming, but excitable.

1948, 1960, 1972, 1984, 1996

OXEN are hardworking and dependable, steady and trustworthy. They like to follow rules.

1949, 1961, 1973, 1985, 1997

TIGERS are powerful, passionate, and daring. They are also rebellious and unpredictable.

1950, 1962, 1974, 1986, 1998

DRAGONS are full of strength and energy and always on the go. They love a colorful life and set high standards in everything they do.

1940, 1952, 1964, 1976, 1988

SNAKES are wise, clever, and soft-spoken. They like good books and deep thoughts. They dress well and are quite vain.

1941, 1953, 1965, 1977, 1989

RABBITS are kind, gentle, polite, and sensitive to beauty. They live to an old age.

1951, 1963, 1975, 1987, 1999

HORSES are very attractive, with a lot of sex appeal. They are talkative and sensitive. They are changeable and fall in love easily.

1942, 1954, 1966, 1978, 1990

MONKEYS are quick-witted and charming, but deceitful. They are inventive and can be successful at almost anything, especially languages.

1944, 1956, 1968, 1980, 1992

SHEEP are tender and sympathetic, often rather shy. They can become rather overwhelmed by life.

1943, 1955, 1967, 1979, 1991

ROOSTERS are a little too sure of themselves. They are proud and handsome. Some roosters talk quickly all the time and are funny; others look at you clearly with hard eyes.

1945, 1957, 1969, 1981, 1993

DOGS are very likeable. They are honest, sincere, loyal, and intelligent and like things to be fair and just.

1946, 1958, 1970, 1982, 1994

PIGS are honest and brave. They can accept the hard things in life and never hold a grudge.

1947, 1959, 1971, 1983, 1995

Things to look for in your library

A Taste of China. Roz Denny (Thomson Learning, 1994).
The Buffalo Boy and the Weaver Girl. Mary Alice Downie (Quarry Press, 1989).
Chinese Fairy Tales (cassette).
Chinese Jump Rope. Sheree S. Marty (Sterling, 1994).
Chinese Migrations. Judith Kendra (Thomson Learning, 1994).
Chinese Opera (video).
Postcards from China. Zoe Dawson (Raintree/Steck Vaughn, 1995).
Red Eggs and Dragon Boats: Celebrating Chinese Festivals. Carol Stepanchuk (Pacific View Press, 1994).
Why Rat Comes First: A Story of the Chinese Zodiac. Clara Yen (Children's Press, 1991).

MAKE A DRAGON KITE

You can make your own dragon kite for Qing Ming Day. Draw your own dragon or use ours for inspiration. Red and yellow are auspicious colors for a dragon—and they make a nice, bright kite!

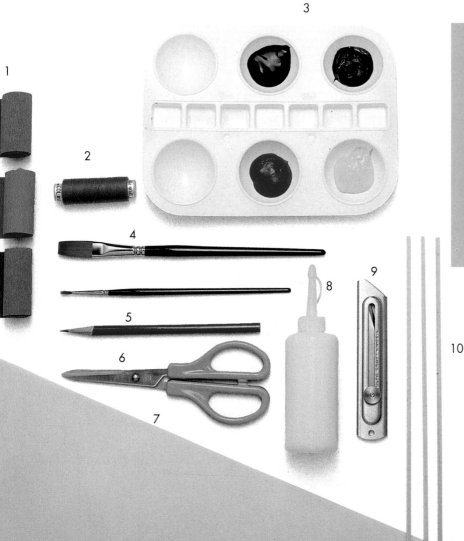

You will need:
1. Crepe paper rolls in three colors
2. Thread
3. Tempera paint
4. Paintbrushes
5. Pencil
6. Scissors
7. Tissue paper
8. Glue
9. Xacto knife
10. Three 13-inch (33-cm) dowels

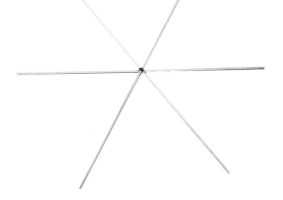

1 Arrange the dowels like this. Use the thread to tie them together in the middle.

2 Carefully cut small slits in the ends of the dowels. (You may need an adult to help with this.)

3 Tie the thread around the edges of the kite, using the slits to hold it in place.

4 Cut the tissue paper to fit around the kite shape with a 1/2-inch (1.3-cm) flap on each edge. Paint a dragon face on it. Lay the frame over the paper. Put glue on the flaps and fold them down.

5 Cut two pieces of thread 8 inches (20 cm) long. Tie them to points A and B. Tie the end of the rest of the thread to the center. Then tie the two short pieces to the long thread to make a harness. Glue crepe paper streamers to the bottom of the kite. You're ready to fly!

MAKE TANG YUAN

T ang Yuan is a sweet dessert that is eaten at the Winter Solstice Festival. It's also offered to ancestors as a symbol of family reunion. Tang Yuan is a popular treat, especially with children, and easy to make. This recipe makes enough for four people.

5

6

4

2

3 and 7

8

1 and 9

You will need:
1. 2 cups (280 g) glutinous rice flour
2. 2 cups (400 g) brown sugar
3. Water
4. Red, green, and yellow food coloring
5. Ladle
6. Wooden spoon
7. Measuring cup
8. Saucepan
9. Large bowl

1 Mix the water and flour together in a bowl.

2 Pick up the dough and knead it for a few minutes.

3 Mix the sugar into 5 cups (1.2 l) of water in a saucepan. Heat the sugar water.

4 Divide the dough into three lumps. Add a different color to each, working it in until the dough is colored all the way through. Make sure you wash your hands before switching lumps!

5 Roll the dough into balls the size of large marbles and drop them into the sugar water. Cook them until they rise to the top. Serve the balls in the syrup. You can eat it hot or cold.

GLOSSARY

ancestor, 16	Family member who came before.
auspicious, 8	Bringing good luck.
Buddhism, 5	A religion started by the Buddha that teaches self-control.
Han Chinese, 5	The main group of people in China.
hongbao, 9	A red envelope with money inside given at New Year.
kumquat, 11	A small, sour, orange fruit.
Lamaism, 24	The Tibetan form of Buddhism.
lunar, 6	Following the phases of the moon.
martial arts, 13	Traditional Asian forms of self-defense.
Mongols, 23	People from Central Asia who conquered most of Asia.
Muslim, 5	A follower of Islam.
Overseas Chinese, 5	A Chinese person who lives outside of China.
pagoda, 23	A tower with roofs that curve upward over each floor.
Taoism, 5	A religion that teaches people to follow the way of the world.

INDEX